STARTING YOUR OWN NON-PROFIT ORGANIZATION

DR. SHANTA BARTON-STUBBS

THE NEW IMAGE YOUTH CENTER

Photo Credit: Reginald Simmons and Shanta Barton-Stubbs

Published by Under Construction Empowerment Services, LLC.
214 South Parramore ave.
Orlando, Fl 32805

ISBN: 978-0-9973297-2-8

Printed in the United States of America

Table of Contents

Introduction

I am Dr. Shanta Barton-Stubbs, the founder of New Image Youth Center. New Image Youth Center, (NIYC), is a 501 (c)(3) non-profit organization. We provide an after school program and summer camp for youth in the Parramore community in Orlando, FL. The New Image Youth Center seeks to prevent its students from continuing the cycles of drugs, gangs, poverty, and delinquent behavior.

The Parramore community is a better place since NIYC has invested in providing education, mentoring and positive activities. When school is over for the day, the children always have a place to come, and you can see them running from every block. During the summertime we provide opportunities for kids to get involved in a range of positive and educational activities. NIYC sessions cover personal and professional character building skills that are applicable in the daily lives of our students. We believe that the experiences that we provide to our youth can be applied to their academics and teachings, thus supporting real changes in their surrounding community.

It has been twelve years since this journey started; a journey that would change the lives of the youth in the Parramore community and beyond. On June 7, 2004, I saw four children outside of my parent's church in the Parramore community of Orlando, FL. The children were fighting, cursing, and acting very wild. Actually, they had a grocery cart basket with no grocery store in site. Two youth were inside the basket while the other two were pushing the basket out of control into oncoming traffic. I yelled and said, "What the heck are you doing?" and called them over to me. I opened up the annex in the church for these children, and on that day New Image Youth Center was created. Now, here we are 12 years later, and we have changed the lives of more than 200 students per year. We have twenty-one of them who are high school graduates, 9 students attending local colleges, and two students attending out of state colleges.

In 2011, we had five graduating students our largest graduating class at that point. One of them that gra-duated is Robertson Bassy, he graduated from Boone High School, and was the first student to leave the Parramore community and attend Morehouse College in 10 years. He graduated from Morehouse College in Atlanta, GA in 2015 and currently attends Auburn Uni-versity as a doctoral student. He has truly been a role model and trailblazer for all who attend New Image Youth Center. In 2013, Montaius Stewart graduated from Jones

High School with honors. He received over $50,000.00 in scholarship money and attended Claflin University in Orangeburg, SC, where he is now a senior. Montaius Stewart, LaSarjane Spates, and Brandon Spates were some of the original eight students here at NIYC. It is nothing short of amazing that we have a Computer Science Major, Computer Engineering Major, Criminal Justice Major, and several Nursing Majors all coming from this one youth center.

In twelve years, our attendance has grown, our facility has changed, and we continue to grow in strength. Our first location was at the Church of Freewill Deliverance in their annex. We know have a functioning kitchen which we use for cooking classes, 2 classrooms, a dance room, a big back yard, a community garden and the annex all to serve the youth. In October of 2010, we started our Community Garden. Our Community Garden has expanded into our Health and Fitness program. Thanks to a grant from the Blue Foundation and several other small foundations, we have been imparting a healthy lifestyle into the lives of our students, their parents, and the community as a whole.

New Image is a 501(c)(3) nonprofit organization. None of our students pay to attend any of our programs. It is nothing short of a miracle on how this program exists. We are not funded by the federal government, but we depend on grants and donations from the public.

NIYC started on the foundation of getting four children off the streets of Parramore. But in twelve years we have touched the lives of more than hundreds of children. One action from one person has evolved into many actions by many people.

It has always been our goal to reach out-side of NIYC and bring awareness to this challenging community. By sharing our insights, foresights, and goals, we hope it will make a difference to those around us.

We want to break the cycle of poverty and bring aware-ness to the community that there is a different path to take By definition, a non-profit organization is an organi-zation with the purpose of which is something other than making a profit and is often dedicated to furthering a particular social cause or advocating for a particular point of view.

There are a lot of good Samaritans out on this earth that have their eye out for the likes of mankind and would want for nothing more than to see it succeed.

Unfortunately, you have those that are less fortunate and need help because they were born without a silver spoon in their mouth. They may have experienced a tragedy in their life and weren't able to recover from it. They may have lost a loved one. They may have parents strung out on drugs. The list is endless, but at the end of the day, the ultimate goal of a non-profit is to raise better people for the restoration of mankind.

Non-Profits provide hope. Non-profits create leaders. Non-profits are made by those who wish to commit to one of the most gratifying acts of the human race; instilling compassion in others. This guide is for anyone who wants to give back to their community or offer a special service to those who are in need. Rather you want to help with veterans, displaced families, pregnant teens or children, this guide will help lead you to what steps you need to take next.

Tip #1
Serve At Your Level of Expertise

This world needs more help. Everyday there is a tragedy that takes place and there is a service which is needed. There are homeless people, children, and families in every state that you go to. Wounded veterans, people losing their jobs, and the hardships continue to go on. It's no secret that this world could use more not-for-profits and people who are willing to give unto others and serve others, as we were born to do. I have seen people who think that it's not their business to help others and I have seen those who want to do more. The reality is, it's all of our jobs to do something. There are so many awesome people who are just waiting to start something amazing.

First of all, I just want to let you know that the timing will never be just right. Stop waiting for a certain time in your life to take place in order for you to give back or for you to do something great for others. While you are waiting, people and children are perishing. The time is now and you are needed now. Start in whatever capacity that you can at this point and as you continue to go on, the resources and the things which you need will begin to find you. What do I mean? Well let me tell you. If you have an idea to provide services or start a not-for-profit organization, then why don't you start now? There are people who need you now. You may not be fully able to work as you intend to with your ultimate plan, but the point is to just get started. Find a location or an organization or someone who can use your level of expertise. Be very open and honest with them about what you want to do and let them know that you would like to start helping them enhance their program in some way.

Now remember that every organization has their own culture so it's very important to be sure that you are able to fit in with what they have already. Talk to the Executive Director about what you would like to do to bring an extra boost to their already existing programs. Try enhancing some of the programs that they already have, remember to be very respectful and also be very open about the insight that you have for your own future organization. By volunteering your time and being dedicated to another organization, you're not only helping in some capacity but also enhancing the programming of that organization by providing the services which you are talented with.

Tip #2
Get In Where You Can Fit In

Now, there may not be a not-for-profit organization that is doing exactly what you would like to do, which is what is going to make you different and unique. Be willing to share your ideas with other people to see if they have any knowledge about how you can get started. Remember that there are some professionals and experts who have already tried some of the things which you want to do, and they may be able to guide you in the areas where you are to go and where you are not to go. Not all advice is good advice; however, it is great to be able to learn from those who have already gone before you. We often hear the phrase, "do not reinvent the wheel" and this is true. Why waste time doing something the hard way when there is an easier way to do it? Save yourself the time and prevent the headache. However, there is a proper and improper way of doing things. I can't tell you how many times I found myself creating something which already existed, if only I knew then what I know NOW!

It may take you some time to learn things, but without it you lack understanding. This is why it is so important for you to surround yourself with someone who is already doing what you're trying to do and learn from their level of expertise. Remember to be open-minded and willing to listen and learn. Let them know upfront that you are there to be a student, and also bring your level of expertise to the table.

For example, I have had individuals who have come to me for consultations and want to talk about their plans of doing something similar to what we are doing at NIYC. Most of the time, they just want us to sit down while I guide them along the way without them actually being able to give back in some way. It's hard as an Executive Director to take time away from your programming, when people are not giving back into the program that they are taking you away from.

By offering your services and volunteering, you are showing that you value their time and in return would like to offer them something back so that it can be a win-win situation for you and the organization.

Tip #3
Value Good Information

Executives Directors are more prone to give you good information when you are willing to invest back into their organization. The great opportunity here is that you get to work and learn at no cost to you. Please be considerate in the process, because remember time is money, and as an Executive Director is taking time for you, they could be working on things to enhance their own program.

It is only fair for you to offer up time as well to show your consideration in the time that they are taking with you. Otherwise, do not be offended if a consultation fee is involved. This leads us to our next point.

Tip #4
Invest in Yourself

If you are trying to learn, please be willing to invest in yourself and your future organization in order to receive the best information and guidance that is possible. Believe me, you may not recognize it now but you are going to need the guidance of someone who has already been there. With the politics of not-for-profit organizations being at an all-time high and the misconception of not-for-profit grant money being available, you must be open-minded in learning from the professionals and the experts.

There are many free opportunities available that you can take advantage of, some of these opportunities may come in the form of classes that are taught at certain universities. Here in Orlando, FL we have the Edyth Bush Institute for Philanthropy at Rollins College which offers a lot of free information for those who are looking to do philanthropy work.

They also offer classes with a tuition fee which would help you receive the information you need specifically for your organization. You must be willing to pay a fee, and pay for the investment that other people are willing to give you. I often tell people that it is very important for you to have a track record of how much you have invested in yourself before asking other people to invest into you and your dreams.

This now leads us to one of the most important tips:

Before any organization, grantor, or sponsor is going to pour into you, he/she will want to know what you have already done.

Tip #5
Build Your Portfolio

This takes us back to our first bit of information. As you are volunteering and doing things to lend a helping hand to other organizations remember to take pictures to record your work. Of course, get permission first and begin to show other people what you are doing. Basically, what you are building at this time is a portfolio. Many people are misunderstood in the concept of grants and think that they are available for anyone who wants to do something good. This could be true or could not be true. You are going to have to present some type of portfolio, or resume showing that you are serious and that you have already started the process. Otherwise, people with all kinds of ideas would be getting grant money; and I am here to tell you that grant money doesn't come this easy. I like to advise people in making sure you maintain all of your receipts, pictures, literature, and any media clippings of what you are doing in order to show people that you are serious and that you have already gotten started in some capacity. This is important to know, and to have because you will have proof to show that you are ready to give back; and that you have already started the process and have been willing to invest in your own organization in order to see it come to pass. Remember to post your pictures and ideas and things on social media so that you can begin to draw in an audience of people who would want to support your cause. This way you are not able to only advertise your goals and missions, but you're also able to attract those like-minded people.

Remember that no one person can fulfill a need solely on their own; it takes a team of dedicated people to make it possible. In my case many people assume that I do a lot of the work myself. Yes, I am the most dedicated in the organization; however, I have a team of people that help make it possible. These people are what we call the Board of Directors, advisors, sponsors, volunteers, or even donors.

Tip #6
Know the Process

At the beginning of your process there are going to be a lot of people who want to jump on board, but it is very important for you to recognize those people who are serious about the mission and those people who you feel may be able to grab on and run with your vision and mission the same way that you would. So as you begin to post and share more about your organization you will be able to filter through those people who need to feel good about something, and the ones who really want to make a difference.

Remember that not every person is designed to be one of your Board of Directors however, there are many positions that you would need to fill; so sit with each person one on one to get an idea of what they would like to help you do.

Tip #7
Consider If You Are
Willing To Give

Contrary to what we may think or see, not-for-profit organizations take a lot of personal money? Think about this:
Are you willing to give what is needed in order to produce
the type of organization that you want to produce? If your
answer is no to this, and you only want other people to
pour into your organization, then maybe you should
rethink your idea. Why you may ask? Its simple, people
are only going to be willing to give as much as you
yourself have been willing to give. People are not going to
be willing to do more then what you have done to invest
in your own organization. So, what does this look like?
Well, do small fund raising things such as carwashes,
bake sales, get-togethers where people are introduced to
your mission and allow them to see that you are not
afraid to work for what you are trying to create. This
perception is needed at the beginning and throughout the
life of your organization. It is very important to show others
that you are invested just as much as you are requesting
them to be invested into your vision.

Tip #8
Be Smart

Be very smart about what you're doing and please, don't expect money to just fall from the sky. Please note that this work that you are getting into will require your hard work now and for the duration of your organization. One of the biggest misconceptions I see is many people wanting to get into not-for-profit work and thinking that they can quit their actual job. Please don't!

Make sure that your organization is stable enough to maintain what is needed in order to take care of a salary as well as overhead. I really want to be honest with you. After 12 years of business I have not yet been able to obtain a salary; however, this has never been my ultimate goal. My goal has always been to work my personal career, but to be sure that I had enough money coming in to take care of my overhead, staff, and organizational programs. I am not saying that you can't get a check from it and that it cannot be done, but I want you to be very open and focused on the importance of the organization prospering rather than the organization taking care of you.

Tip #9
Prepare for Upfront Work

Now, after you have begun to do all of the forefront work, you may now be ready to start the actual organization. The IRS not-for-profit process is not the easiest process and can take years to complete.

With New Image Youth Center, it took us over four years to become our own not-for-profit organization. But here are a few things you can do while in the process of waiting to get started.

Tip #10
Join Forces

Research and see if there's an organization that can use your resources and ideas to help enhance their own program. This way, they may be willing to add you on as a program or even put you under the umbrella of their not-for-profit status. This is the easiest way to get started as you will have the guidance and the credentials to benefit as a not-for-profit organization. New Image Youth Center did this for years.

This process can teach you the ins and outs of 501 (c)(3)s, which you will need as you begin to learn the process on your own. At times not-for-profit organizations are willing to do this in exchange for a fee, a grant, or your talents for running one of their programs. In return you will have the protection that you need as a not-for-profit organization and the two of you can begin to support the cause together.

Team work is needed when you are trying to fulfill your needs. Now this would not ultimately be your call, however it is a great way to get started without having to cover the overhead yourself.

Tip #11
Hire Out If Needed

Now a lot of people are capable of doing the application for the IRS paperwork on their own. I personally hired someone to help in the process, because I recognized that it was more than what I understood at the time. You will not only need your basic mission and vision, but you will also need the information for your Board of Directors, your bylaws, and other things which they're going to ask for. My best advice in this process is: if you are not a good writer, then consult and hire someone to do it for you. But, if you feel comfortable doing it yourself then you can also go through the process as an IRS representative will guide you along the way. But, be knowledgeable in what is expected before you get started

Tip #12
Draft a Mission Statement

An organization's mission statement should clearly communicate what it is that they do. Many mission statements succumb to over use of words in general. Good mission statements should be clear, memorable, and concise. Some should also add "inspiring" to the list of descriptors. Find a standard of individual things that relate to your organization and this often ends up as being part of the mission. The NIYC mission is:

New Image Youth Center aims to improve the lives of youth by providing an environment where students feel safe to dream, and to support the realization of dreams through programs designed to foster academic, social, and physical well-being.

How to Write a Mission Statement

A mission statement which is well developed can be a great tool for understanding, developing, and communicating fundamental business objectives, and should be expressed properly.

Examples:

- What does your organization do?
- What does it stand for?
- And why does your organization do it?
- What target audiences are you serving?
- What benefits do you offer them?
- Do you solve a problem for your clients?
- What type of work environment do you want for your employees?

The Process for Developing a Mission Statement:

1. Start with Your Imagination
You can Imagine what an organization can do, and then use your creativity and develop into reality and make it trustworthy.

2. Make Unique Policies
Don't undervalue your business.

3. Review, Revise
Mission statements serve multiple functions, for the rest of your business's life. So, review and revise it, if needed.

Also, remember your mission statement should be reviewed and revised as necessary, because changes are constant with not-for-profits.

I have been told that our mission statement is too long and we recently created a simple but unique tagline which sums up what we do in a few words.

So, mission statements vary from organization to organization and may be different from time to time. Be sure to create something which satisfies the reason your organization exist.

Tip #13
Stick to Your Mission

Nonprofit organizations must devote their resources to the charitable purposes and activities that were identified in the IRS application. Not-for-profit organizations should not intentionally drift away from their original purpose and activities. Also, sometimes organizations make an intentional decision to change their purposes and activities. This is allowed as long as it is reported and changed with IRS. Before making any changes, check and make sure that the new purpose and activities will not create problems with what you have already established.

Be sure to think over the process before doing it and consult with your Board of Directors. There was once a time when we at New Image Youth Center were having a hard time maintaining our overhead. Another not-for-profit organization came along to assist us. However, their plan of assisting us was getting us to participate with their mission and having all of our contacts and donors to support a mission which was different from our norm. Although we needed the money and the guidance, we had to turn that opportunity down since it was not a part of the services that we provided. So, always remember to stick to your vision or you will fall for anything.

Tip #14
Know the Law

Governmental Rules.

A not-for-profit organization is allowed to give tax receipts for donations they receive. Nonprofit organiza-tions are able to issue an official donation receipt for income tax purposes, and this is often seen as one of the main advantages. People and businesses that donate and get these receipts can use them to reduce the income tax that they owe to the government. The government in return gives tax breaks to individuals each year with the money they would have normally collected. The govern-ment has there-fore made rules to ensure that nonprofit organizations are collecting donations, issuing receipts and carrying out activities for charity purposes. These receipts can reduce the income tax owed by people or businesses that donate to the nonprofit organization, so that they can encourage donations. However, there is no legal requirement for a foundation to issue receipts for donations. Issuing receipts involves an administrative burden, so some foundations decide not to issue them.

Tip #15
Maintain Control over
Your Activities

You can carry out your own activities either by using a staff, volunteers or by working with outside individuals and groups. When you are working with outside individuals and groups, you must maintain direction and control over the use of the resources, and be able to demonstrate this direction and control. Make sure that everyone is aware of the mission and the vision of your organization and that all involved have the same common goal. Oversee what is being done, as what is being done reflects your organization.

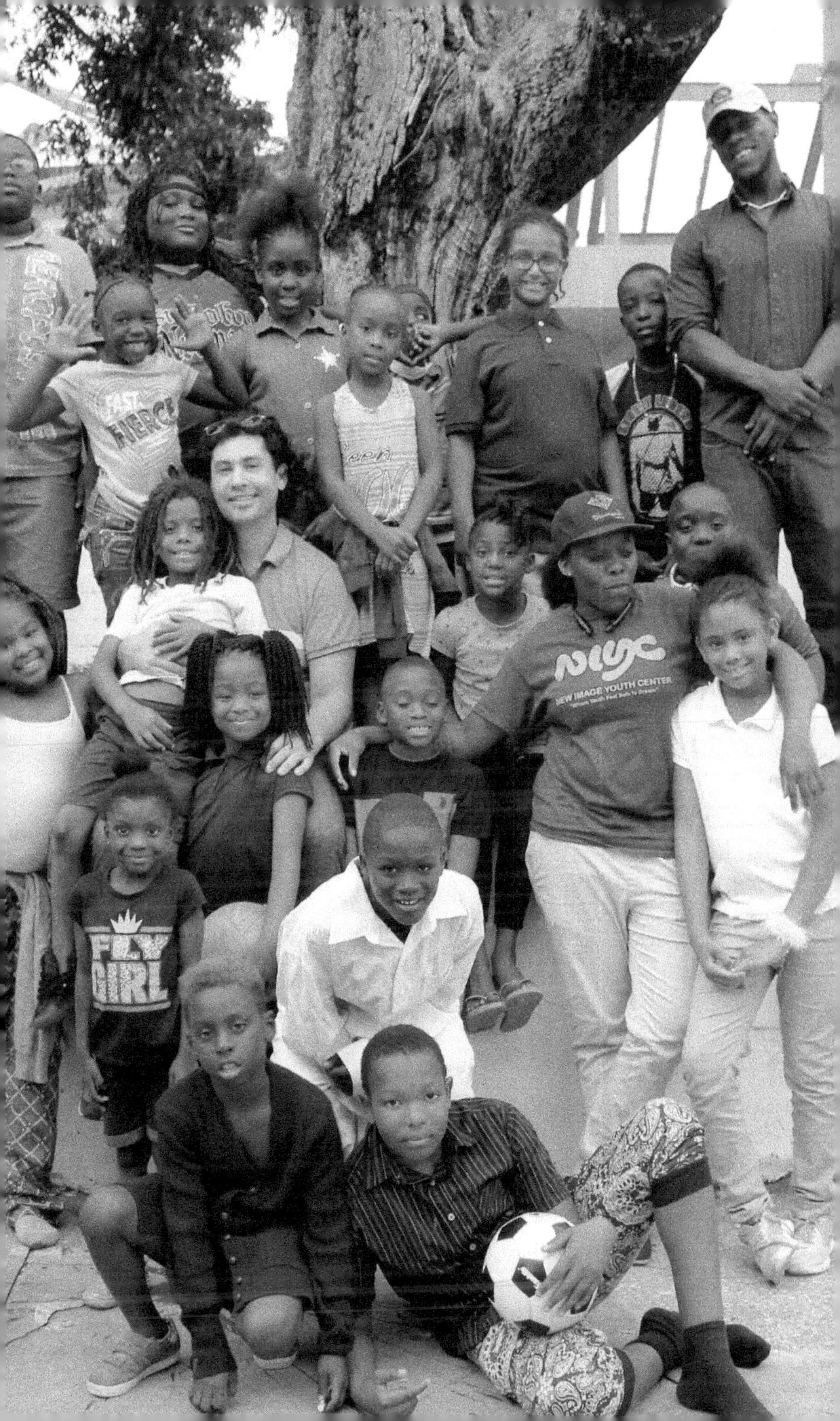
NIYC
NEW IMAGE YOUTH CENTER
FLY GIRL

Tip #16
Avoid Political Activities, You are Not the President

Nonprofit Organizations cannot have political purposes, or political activities. "Purposes," are the reasons for which an organization is created. "Activities," are the programs and projects an organization uses to achieve its purposes.

For example: A non-profit organization cannot:

- Publish an article in its newsletter supporting the re-election of a candidate who shares a position on an issue that the organization is facing.
- Hand out pamphlets during an election campaign that proposes certain laws (but, it would be acceptable if the pamphlet mentioned politicians from all parties).
- Invite two candidates to speak at its annual meeting, but give one candidate more time to speak or to endorse one of them.

Tip #17
Keep Records

Every not-for-profit organization should keep records of their financial statements, bank statements, income tax records, expense accounts, copies of official donation receipts, governing documents, (constitution, trust document, letters patent, etc.), minutes of meetings, annual reports, annual information forms, accounting ledgers, fundraising materials and written agreements. This also include purchase orders, receipts, bank deposit slips, invoices, cancelled checks, credit card receipts, work orders, delivery slips, emails and correspondence.

Tip #18
Count Your Money and
Use It Wisely

Only money that is spent directly on your nonprofit organization's activities, (for example, providing educational scholarships) or gifts counts toward meeting the success of the organization. Paying salaries for the people who are actually doing organizational work and buying equipment used in organization activities also counts toward meeting the success of your organization.

Spending on activities that do not directly accomplish your nonprofit organization's purpose does not count towards the budget. This too should all be recorded as mentioned above.

Tip #19
Treat Your Nonprofit
Like a Business

A not-for-profit is like a business. It has a Board of Directors, marketing and human resource departments, and decision-making executives, all geared towards understanding the market for not-for-profits and making day-to-day choices that ultimately help us to be more competitive and successful.

These groups develop strategic plans, keep financial records and audits, and monitor compliance. So, why treat it any differently than how you would treat a for profit organization? Just because we are not in it to make a profit, does not mean it is not a BUSINESS!

For nonprofits, it is important to invest in key aspects of the organization, just as any business does to help it grow and prosper. When a business does well, consumers immediately see the value of purchasing its product or service. When a nonprofit does well, donors immediately see the rewards of doing something good and want to donate, (you should ask NIYC about their book for reasons to give).

In closing, not-for-profits are changing lives across the world, and we have a responsibility to continue thinking of ways to excel in order to grow and to become the best at what we do. But, real change can only be accomplished if we modify the way we think about how nonprofits should, "invest" their resources while making a mark for themselves. Let's not limit the scale of their dreams; instead, let's help.

Tip #20
Be a walking / talking Billboard

Whether you are supporting your own organization or supporting a cause you believe in, you should always be willing to share the mission with others wherever you may be. Post things on your social media page highlighting the cause and invite others to be a part of it. While standing in the line of a grocery store, tell others what you are doing and how that mission makes a difference for the community you serve. Always be prepared to show and tell others why you became involved. I have done this so many times before and found some great resources and donors for New Image Youth Center just by being a walking billboard. You should always be ready to share the mission of the organization and this is one of the cheapest and easiest ways to advertise which is also known as "word of mouth marketing". Word of mouth is a powerful tool in many ways because people come trust their friends. For example, would you go see a movie that a friend told you about or a movie based on what a couple of reviews say online? Exactly. People operate that way with anything because they trust their friends. By being a walking billboard, you will be able to extend your network, increase your reach, and allow your business to be carried by the most powerful form of advertising.

All in all, creating a non-profit requires a lot of hard work and dedication to come to fruition. Most often times, people lack the tools necessary to start a non-profit. I'm not talking about a staff, money, a vision, or anything of that sort. They lack leadership qualities, communication skills, and more often than not, they don't have the right motivation to start a not-for-profit organization. A major pillar of becoming the head of a non-profit is growing as a person. Running your own organization forces you to grow into the person necessary to run it; more importantly it is a learning experience.

Through these tips, I hoped to have accomplished the task of allowing you new insight on what is necessary for you to get started with your own non-profit organization. It is not an easy challenge. It is by no means a hobby that you should just pick up in your spare time. Running a non-profit is something that requires your mind, body, and soul and it is something that requires an objective to be successful. What do I mean by successful? In order to impact the lives of hundreds, even thousands of people, there has to be a system in place and an objective to reach for. Running a non-profit is similar to having a relationship; it takes hard work and constant adaptation. You are always learning. The good news? Running a non-profit is the most rewarding and prospering experience that one can experience. It provides your life with purpose. More importantly, you will be subject to being accountable for the plethora of lives you manage to impact through your unselfish acts of kindness and unforgiving amounts of support you provide for the people who aren't as fortunate as others. Be the light at the end of their tunnel. Be the change you wish to see in the world.

Thank You

Thank you for taking the time to read the tips and hints of So you want to start a Non Profit? Let's do some homework first! We hope that this information has helped you in some way decide what to do and how to do it. If you are ever in need of further information or consultations please don't hesitate to contact us on our website at www.newimageyouth.org. We are also available for speaking engagements, conferences, webinars and more.